GET

YOUR FUTURE DEPENDS ON IT!

Author, Mission Advisor
Carlos Moreno

Executive Producer, Author
Elliot Washor

Creative Advisor
Isabella A. Moreno

Executive Creative Director & Character Designer
Peter Reynolds

Executive Producer
Paul Reynolds

Creative Director
Leigh Hallisey

Storyboard & Production Designer
Bob Flynn

Production Designers
Christina Kelly
Vath Doangpratheep

Producer
Mikaela Johnson

Print Preparation
Studiowink

Focus Group and Reviews
Special thanks to:
Owen Purcell
Casey Lamb

Bella, a teen with a passion for tinkering, building, and working with her hands, was busy working in the basement workshop of her family's apartment building. She was so focused on her latest project—a solar-powered drone—she almost didn't hear her mom calling from upstairs.

BELLA...YOUR COUSIN XAVIER WILL BE HERE IN A FEW MINUTES!

REMEMBER, HE'S VISITING FOR SPRING VACATION, AND I KNOW HE'D LOVE TO SEE YOUR PROJECT.

MOM, I'VE GOT ZERO TIME FOR DISTRACTIONS! I'VE BEEN ONLINE WITH MY MENTOR MR. PAPI, AND I NEED TO SHOW THIS DRONE PROTOTYPE TO HIM NEXT WEEK.

RIGHT NOW IT'S BASICALLY A PILE OF JUNK WITH A COUPLE OF WINGS POKING OUT.

MY FUTURE AS A SOLAR TECHNICIAN IS ON THE LINE HERE!

Bella's mom poked her head into the basement.

BELLA, BELLA... MY BRIGHT, CLEVER, GENEROUS DAUGHTER.

XAVI LOOKS UP TO YOU, AND HE'S HAVING A TOUGH TIME IN SCHOOL.

HE COULD USE SOME INSPIRATION TO HELP HIM GET BACK ON TRACK, AND YOU ARE SO INSPIRING WHEN YOU TALK ABOUT YOUR PROJECTS.

SO, PLEASE? FOR XAVI? AND YOUR MOM?

AND, UM, YOUR DOG, MARLEY?

Marley barked at the sound of his name, and Bella giggled before remembering she was annoyed.

OKAY, FINE, MOM.

BUT IF I'M GIVING UP PROJECT TIME, XAVI'S ON SNACK-RUN DUTY. I'LL MAKE HIM A LIST OF ACCEPTABLE SNACK CHOICES AND DELIVERY TIMES.

A few minutes later...

STOMP

STOMP

STOMP

BELLA!

GUESS WHAT I HAVE?

HMMM, HOLD UP...GIVE ME A SEC, WHAT COULD IT POSSIBLY BE?

She liked teasing her cousin, but the truth was she really loved Xavier's comic books. She was super impressed with Xavi—at fourteen he'd already launched his own comic book publishing company, with the help of their Aunt Nia and her print shop.

And Xavier was one of Bella's biggest fans. Xavier really admired Bella, whose loss of vision in one eye never clouded her vision of what's possible. She was always building new inventions made from materials she found at the recycling center and salvage business next door.

Xavier bowed theatrically.

IF IT PLEASES HER ROYAL INVENTOR EXTRAORDINAIRE, CHECK OUT MY NEWEST COMIC BOOK!

Xavier spread the comic book on Bella's workbench and began sharing.

SO THE MAIN CHARACTER IS CEDRIC. HE'S LIKE A REGULAR KID AT SCHOOL WHO ACCIDENTALLY DISCOVERS A MAGIC APP, CALLED SCHOOL-AR, ON HIS SMARTPHONE.

IT'S LIKE CEDRIC HAS A MAGIC WAND. COULD BE AWESOME, OR, IT COULD CAUSE SOME MAJOR DRAMA IN THE WRONG HANDS.

NO WORRIES, CEDRIC IS THE MAN!

HE'S ALL ABOUT USING THE POWER FOR GOOD.

SEE HERE? HE MAKES HIS FIRST SCHOOL-AR ZAP, AND CHECK OUT WHAT HAPPENS.

blah blah blah blah blah..

cedric

ZAP!

HMM, I LOVE WORKING WITH MY HANDS... RACING CARS... FIXING THINGS.

RIGHT, THOSE ARE THINGS THAT MAKE YOU HAPPY.

YEAH, BUT WHAT DOES THAT HAVE TO DO WITH SCHOOL?

WELL—IT HAS EVERYTHING TO DO WITH LEARNING.

IF THAT'S YOUR SPARK—IF THAT'S WHO YOU ARE...

...THEN OPEN THIS DOOR...

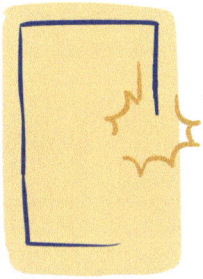
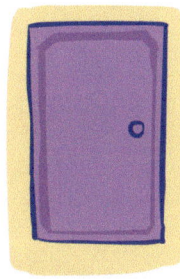

...AND GO EXPLORE A PATHWAY TO THE SKILLED TRADES.

GET REAL...

SAME OLD SCHOOL

COME ON CEDRIC—DON'T BE LATE—YOU NEED TO GET INSIDE BEFORE CLASS STARTS!

ZAP!

CALLING ALL LEARNERS Learn Outside!

REAL WORLD LEARNING THIS WAY

MEANWHILE...

TEXTBOOKS ARE TEXT-BORING! MY TEACHER SEEMS TO THINK READING IS THE BEST AND ONLY WAY TO LEARN. I LEARN BEST BY DOING, BUILDING, OR WORKING WITH OTHERS...THESE WORKSHEETS AND QUIZZES DON'T SHOW WHAT I KNOW OR WHAT I CAN DO!

ZAP!

HI CEDRIC, I'M LEON—I'LL BE YOUR MENTOR AT ACE RACERS.

IT'LL BE A LOT OF HARD, HANDS-ON WORK, BUT YOU'LL GET IT! PUT YOUR MATH AND SCIENCE SKILLS TO WORK, AND YOU'LL LEARN A LOT.

SPEEDING RIGHT ALONG...

WHY IS COLLEGE MY ONLY PATH?

CAREER CENTER

GUIDANCE COUNSELOR

COLLEGE

TIME TO ZAP THAT OLD SCENE!

ZAAPP!

Apprenticeships!

COLLEGE

Trade Certification

WHEN STUDENTS' JOURNEYS ARE SUPPORTED THE RIGHT WAY, IT LEADS TO SUCCESS—AND CHANCES TO GIVE BACK!

YEARS LATER...

deed

MORTGAGE PAID!

MENTOR CENTER!

THERE ARE ALREADY SCHOOLS THAT KNOW HOW IMPORTANT IT IS TO LEARN ONLINE; TO BUILD STUFF WITH YOUR HANDS; TO HAVE TEACHERS WHO ARE COOL AND PASSIONATE ABOUT THE THINGS YOU LOVE, AND WHO CONNECT YOU WITH PEOPLE IN THE COMMUNITY WHO CAN HELP MAKE YOUR SKILLS EVEN STRONGER.

I REALLY WANT TO BELIEVE YOU, BELLA!

BUT I ALSO DON'T WANT TO GET MY HOPES UP AND THEN FIND MYSELF RIGHT BACK IN MY SEAT AT MY REGULAR OL' SCHOOL.

NOT ONLY CAN I PROMISE YOU THESE SCHOOLS EXIST, I CAN SHOW ONE TO YOU.

IN FACT, AUNTIE SYLVIE AND UNCLE SEYMOUR STARTED A SCHOOL JUST LIKE THAT, AND I'M A STUDENT THERE.

Xavi didn't look convinced.

YOU HAVE TO BELIEVE ME, XAVI. OUR SCHOOL HELPS YOU DISCOVER AND APPLY THE REAL YOU, GET THE SUPPORT YOU NEED TO FEEL GOOD ABOUT YOURSELF AND YOUR TALENTS, AND TO BECOME A REAL SUCCESS.

MY SCHOOL ISN'T ASKING ME WHO THE **REAL** ME IS. I'M NOT EVEN SURE MY PARENTS KNOW THE REAL ME.

THEY'RE STUCK ON THIS IDEA THAT I HAVE TO GO TO COLLEGE TO GET A REAL JOB. BUT THAT'S NOT WHO I AM—OR HOW I WANT TO GET TO THE REAL ME.

I KNOW I'M LUCKY,

MY PARENTS HAVE ALWAYS CARED ABOUT WHO I AM, NOT JUST WHO THEY WANTED ME TO BE—TRUST ME, I KNOW IT'S NOT LIKE THAT IN EVERY FAMILY,

WITHOUT TELLING ME WHAT TO DO, THEY LISTENED AND SUPPORTED ME, EVEN WHEN I WAS STRUGGLING.

BELLA—**GET REAL,** NO WAY A SCHOOL CAN REALLY BE LIKE THAT.

BUT XAVI, DON'T YOU SEE— **IT IS REAL!**

THE SCHOOL THEY BUILT IS HELPING ME NAVIGATE MY WAY TO WHO I WANT TO BECOME. BUT, I'LL ADMIT—IT'S NOT EASY.

She looked at Xavier, her expression serious.

IT'S A LOT OF HARD WORK, REAL WORLD WORK, WITH REAL WORLD RISKS AND REWARDS.

WHAT DOES THAT EVEN MEAN?

THAT'S WHAT MY MENTOR, MR. PAPI, TAUGHT ME.

MY SCHOOL HELPED ME FIND—AND LET ME CHOOSE—AN AWESOME MENTOR, MR. PAPI, AT A SOLAR DESIGN, FABRICATION AND INSTALLATION COMPANY RIGHT HERE IN THE CITY.

NOT ONLY AM I LEARNING SOME REALLY USEFUL, FABRICATION AND HIGH-TECH SKILLS, I'M ALSO LEARNING ABOUT WHAT IT MEANS TO WORK IN A REAL COMPANY AND BE PART OF A PROJECT TEAM; LEARNING TO WORK CLOSELY WITH ADULTS —MAKES ME FEEL LIKE A REAL PROFESSIONAL.

Xavier looked down at his sneakers, frustration and anger flashed in his eyes.

WELL, THAT'S ALL GOOD FOR YOU, BELLA, BUT I'M STUCK!

OF COURSE I WISH ALL SCHOOLS WERE LIKE THAT— AND THAT ALL PARENTS LISTENED AND TRIED TO SEE THEIR KIDS FOR WHO THEY REALLY ARE. MY PARENTS DON'T KNOW THAT MY ART IS A BIG PART OF WHO I AM. THEY WANT ME TO GO TO COLLEGE TO BE SOMETHING I DON'T HAVE ANY INTEREST IN.

WELL, WHAT DO THEY WANT YOU TO DO?

THEY THINK I SHOULD BE A LAWYER

THEY HONESTLY THINK LAW SCHOOL IS MY ROAD TO SUCCESS, BUT THAT'S NOT MY JOURNEY.

AT MY SCHOOL IT'S ALL BOOKS AND SUBJECTS THAT AREN'T INTERESTING TO ME, AND TAUGHT BY TEACHERS WHO DON'T KNOW ME. AND COLLEGE AND LAW SCHOOL WOULD JUST BE MORE OF THE SAME.

IT'S SUPER DEPRESSING.

SO, XAVI, THAT CHARACTER IN YOUR COMIC BOOK...IS YOU?

YEAH.

SIGH

I GUESS IT IS.

Suddenly Bella perked up.

HERE'S THE THING. YOUR SUPERPOWER IS SHAPING REALITY WITH ART AND WORDS. MY SUPERPOWER IS BUILDING SOMETHING FROM NOTHING WITH MY HANDS. WE ARE AN UNSTOPPABLE FORCE OF CREATIVITY, AND WE CAN FIX THIS TOGETHER!

And so they did.

Bella and Xavier spent their spring vacation week working, both together and online. Xavi created a comic book to tell the story of how amazing a school can be that respects and taps into students' interests, offers hands-on learning, and matches students with mentors who support and believe in them.

He called their Aunt Nia at the graphic design shop, who was thrilled to print lots and lots of copies.

Meanwhile, Bella worked with her mentor Papi and his company to build a fleet of solar-powered drones to deliver copies of the comic across Xavier's whole city.

On a sunny day later that week, the drones were loaded up and launched.

WRRRR

RR

The comic books were delivered to parents, school administrators, and community leaders at City Hall.

People were finally getting the message, in more ways than one.

EPILOGUE

The Mayor and school leaders were so impressed with Xavier and Bella's work and mission that they could no longer deny how successful this model of learning could be. They worked quickly to transform the city's schools, with the help of Sylvie and Seymour, and Xavier and Bella, too. In the coming years, schools all around the country transformed the way they taught and what and how students learned.

And how did Xavi and Bella end up doing? Xavi transferred to a different school, earned his high school diploma, and went on to receive certifications in graphic design and business. He started a non-profit design and print shop for community action projects. He never forgot his mentor who helped him along the way, and as an alumni was inspired to become a mentor himself to other students at the high school he graduated from, helping each one navigate their way to their REAL potential.

Bella was also wildly successful, as if anyone doubted that. From her interest in visual optics, she invented (and holds the patent for) a new lens to increase solar power efficiency in the apartments she grew up in, as well as in dwellings all over the globe. But she's not done dreaming and building yet, you can be sure.

The End

"If you can be the best, then why not try to be the best?"

Garrett Morgan

"Success is liking yourself, liking what you do, and liking how you do it."

Maya Angelou

It is our vision that all students live lives of their own design, supported by caring mentors and equitable opportunities to achieve their greatest potential. We move forward prepared to activate the power of schools, systems & education through student-directed, real-world learning. We are activists.

"Every student should have the chance to explore multiple pathways, including attending college, earning a two-year degree or industry certificate, pursuing an apprenticeship or finding a job right after graduation. College and career should never be an either-or, especially not as we face unprecedented economic uncertainty and dislocation. We need to maximize opportunity for the students and families who need it most, and high school skilled trades education is one critical way to do that."

- Danny Corwin, Executive Director of Harbor Freight Tools for Schools

Did you know?

- 72 percent of students say high schools could do a better job of giving them chances to learn real-world skills.

- 8 in 10 voters support more funding for high school skilled trades education.

- 80 percent of voters described the trades as "important".

Learn the data: http://harborfreighttoolsforschools.org

For More:

- Big Picture
  https://www.bigpicture.org

- Harbor Freight Fellows
  http://www.harborfreightfellows.org

- Project InSight
  https://www.projectinsightfellows.org

- Fox Giving
  https://www.foxgiving.org

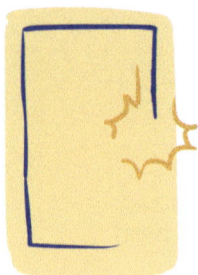

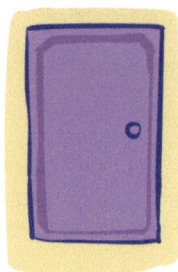

About the authors

Carlos Moreno is the Co-Executive Director of Big Picture Learning. Carlos is a passionate author and educational leader committed to supporting school and system leaders who are creating equitable, high-quality, innovative schools. Carlos is an author and speaker, but is happiest as a roll-up-your-sleeves, "let's get it done" expert practitioner in designing highly engaging schools and environments for youth, particularly those who have and continue to be kept furthest from opportunities.

Elliot Washor is a co-founder of BPL and the Met. He works with school systems and communities all over the world to have every student's interest front and center to achieve equity through access to adults who know they are smart in the many ways that school must start to count.

OUTLEARNERS
OUTLEARN
BY GOING
OUT
TO LEARN

Navigating Our Way

More resources to navigate the CTE/Trades:
www.navigatingourway.org

BIG PICTURE LEARNING

© 2019 BIG PICTURE LEARNING & FABLEVISION Permission granted to copy for non-commercial use & license under CREATIVE COMMONS www.creativecommons.org

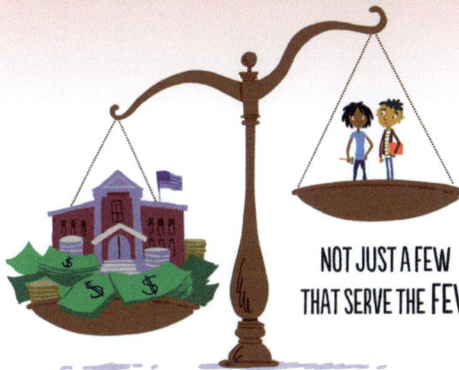

ALL SCHOOLS MUST
BE THE BEST SCHOOLS.

NOT JUST A FEW
THAT SERVE THE FEW.

Navigating Our Way

More resources to navigate the CTE/Trades:
www.navigatingourway.org

BIG PICTURE LEARNING

© 2019 BIG PICTURE LEARNING & FABLEVISION Permission granted to copy for non-commercial use & license under CREATIVE COMMONS www.creativecommons.org